Quacky Careers

What to do with the rest of your life

by Will Bullas

pen-guins...

THE GREENWICH WORKSHOP PRESS

🦉 A GREENWICH WORKSHOP PRESS BOOK

Copyright ©2002 by The Greenwich Workshop Press
All art ©Will Bullas

Published by the Greenwich Workshop Press. One Greenwich Place, P.O. Box 875, Shelton, CT 06484.
(203) 925-0131 or (800) 243-4246.

Library of Congress Cataloging-in-Publication Data
Bullas, Will, 1949-
        Quacky careers: what to do with the rest of your life / by Will Bullas
            p. cm.
ISBN 0-86713-070-9 (alk. paper)
            1. Vocational guidance--United States. 2. Occupations--United States.
3. Professions--United States. I. Title

HF5382.5.U5 B85 2001
331.7'02'0973--dc21
                                        2001040306

Limited edition prints and canvas reproductions, and figurines based on Will Bullas' paintings, are available
exclusively through The Greenwich Workshop, Inc. and its 1200 dealers in North America. Collectors interested
in obtaining information on available releases and the location of their nearest dealer are requested to visit our
website at **www.greenwichworkshop.com** or to write or call the publisher at the address above.

Jacket front: *a class act...*
Book design by Sheryl P. Kober
Printed in Singapore by Imago
First Printing 2002
1 2 3 4 5   04 03 02

What's Your Calling?

Attention all next-generation nervous job seekers and mid-life motivated career changers! Whether you are a *chick with brains…*or *the rocket scientist* in the making, it takes more than a crackerjack resume and computer to find your life's work. The sweaty-palmed interview awaits you!

Put a little smile into your arduous search for the perfect job. Give your quest a rest! Set your resume aside and take a moment to acquaint yourself with a few characters that will surely help to fine-tune your job-hunting strategies.

head of the class…

the prima donna...

a chick with brains...

the rocket

scientist...

how does you garden grow...?

the consultant...

madame porcini...

don quixote...

pen-guins

the ductor...

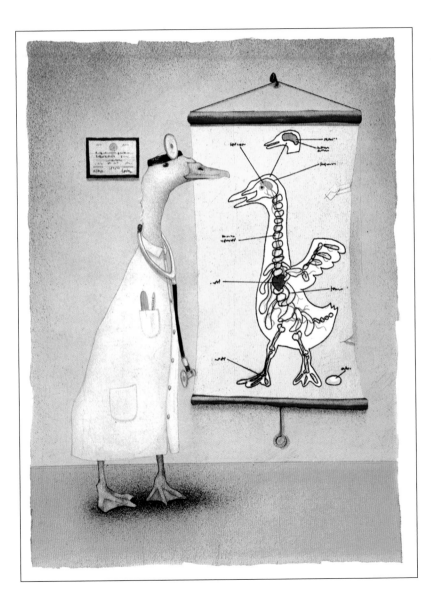

the nurse...

the
dentist...

the cocky eye doc...

space
cadet...

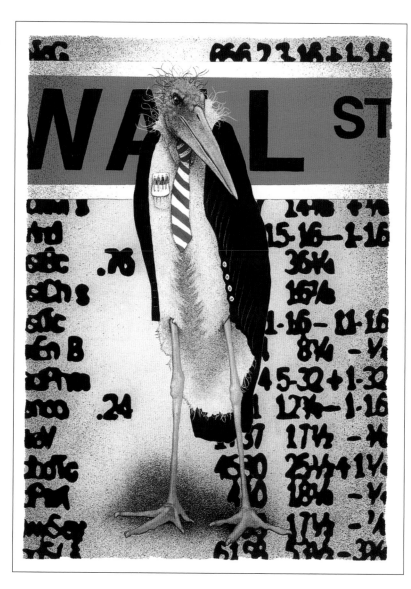

the

storkbroker...

the bar exam...

quid pro crow...

paralegals...

holme boy...

the cat burglar...

secret agent...

monkey business...

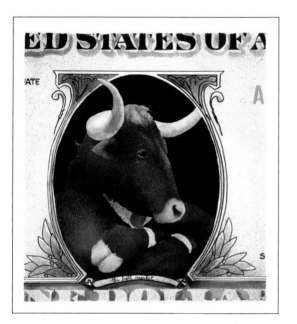 

the stockboys...

THE
ATES
OF A
DER
PRIVATE
F 6
WA
22 B
SERIES
1949
-VULTURE CAPITALIST-

oui, oui monsieur...

the vulture capitalist...

livin' large...

Captain Duck "Thunder" Jones...

the grand finale...

trick rider...

friday's after five...